O.M.I.T.

OVERCOMING MARITAL ISSUES TOGETHER

PASTOR DAMEON L. CUNNINGHAM

www.TrueVinePublishing.org

O.M.I.T.
Dameon L. Cunningham

Published by
True Vine Publishing Co.
P.O. Box 22448
Nashville, TN 37202

ISBN: 978-1-956469-49-3 Paperback
ISBN: 978-1-956469-50-9 eBook

Unless otherwise indicated, all Scripture quotations are from The Holy Bible, King James Version (KJV)

DEDICATION
IN LOVING MEMORY OF

I dedicate this book to the lovely memory of my beloved father and mother, Donald Reed Cunningham and Angie Deniece Wright-Cunningham. Two souls gone too soon. I wasn't able to see their love for each other through matrimony because of the short life they had together. However, I thank God for blessing their union with four amazing children. Without them, there would be no me. I also dedicate this book in memory of my oldest brother, Demetric Lavon Wright. He was known as "D Wright" to others, but I call him Mechie. When my dad departed from this world, Mechie took on the mantle of being a type of father figure to me. He protected me and had my back no matter what. I miss him dearly. I'm often comforted by the memories and dreams I have of him. I'm grateful to have heard him tell me that he was proud of me before cancer claimed his young life at the age of 38 years old. Last but not least, I dedicate this book to the memory of my godmother, Inez Lee. She was the closest I ever got to having a real mother. She had no children of her own biologically, but she loved me like she was the one that birthed me. Lord knows that I wish she was around to see what I've become. I know that she would definitely be proud of me.

Dedication cont.

I can't leave this section without also dedicating this book to my beautiful wife, Brittany Cole-Cunningham. Thank you, baby, for saying yes to my proposal. We were both young and ignorant but willing to step out and be adventurous with our love. Without you, I wouldn't have this experience. We've laughed, we've cried, we've fought, we've danced, we've failed, we've loved, we've lost, and we've gained. It's been a real roller-coaster ride, but I thank God that He allowed me to use some of our story and experiences to help others in matrimony. I love you, baby! Thank you for approving this book.

PRELUDE

M arriage is a wonderful institution ordained by God. If handled appropriately, the two involved will experience great happiness and fulfillment together. It has been said that "your spouse is not the one you dated." This statement is very true. You don't see all the characteristics of people while courting (unless you court for decades); you basically see people at their best. Most of the time, that best is what makes you propose or makes you say, "Yes!" and "I do!" However, after the honeymoon is over and everything has settled, you will eventually see your spouse's imperfections. Be mindful not to point fingers too fast because as you notice your spouse's faults, your spouse will also notice yours. People are unique. They come from various cultures, environments, and upbringings, etc. Therefore, due to these differences, clashing is likely to occur, and as a result, tension will usually rise in the union. The true challenge of handling the conflicts will be first deciding to be up for taking on the challenge of handling the conflicts. Some couples give up too quickly, without putting up the fight to save their union. There are some things that you think are big things right now, but they won't be years from now. The objective is to find out what those things are very early in the marriage so that you won't make mountains out of molehills. In doing so, you will save yourself and your spouse from a lot of unnecessary arguments, stress, and resentment. Believe it or not, some people will experience an ideal marriage from the beginning and throughout their time with one another. However, that's not the case for everyone. If you find that you are within the percentage of those that experience turbulence within marriage, this book may be a great resource for you. O.M.I.T. offers universal, practical godly principles. If applied correctly and sincerely, the couple will more than likely be able to alleviate and annihilate the common issues that plague marriages today. This tool offers insights and personal experiences that will help couples maximize their happiness with one another and increase their love for each other while working through difficult times. As I stated, this is a tool and should not take the place of professional couple's therapy when needed. Please get professional help when necessary.

TABLE OF CONTENTS

CHAPTER ONE:
Newly Wedded/ Initial Years

1

B eing newly wedded is undoubtedly one of the happiest times for couples. You get to take your honey to the moon—on a honeymoon, that is. It is an exclusive vacation spent together by a couple that has been newly wedded. The honeymoon usually takes place immediately following the wedding or a short period after it. Couples should enjoy their honeymoon to the fullest. Every newly wedded couple should experience some form of honeymoon. Whether they last a weekend, a week, or a month, honeymoons can be essential in establishing that initial bond between the two lovers. The honeymoon will give you the time to explore one another on a high level of intimacy. Utilize this time to see your limits but be careful not to push them. It is possible during this time to find out what you and your partner really enjoy as far as sex, romance, and affection go. Be mindful to pay close attention to your mate during this time. You may not only learn what your spouse is willing to do for you, you may also learn what you are willing to do for your spouse.

Although the honeymoon may be a time of spontaneous blissful endeavors, if not careful, the honeymoon may be the beginning and end of excitement for some. Many couples mistakenly think that their new life together may go as it did on the vacation. However, they are met with a rude awakening when they see how their two different lifestyles begin to clash. I would like to think that you and your spouse have participated in some kind of premarital counseling. Premarital counseling should give the couple prudent, practical, and pious advice. It is very common for couples to have counseling sessions with the minister who will perform the marriage ceremony. However, it is not uncommon to seek counsel from licensed family therapists. I recommend premarital counseling because it will help prepare couples for the possible twists and turns that married life can present. Make no mistake about it, you may not be fully prepared but at least you will have an idea about some of the things that can and will surface.

Once the "I do's" have been declared and the smoke of the honeymoon has cleared, you will find yourself in the initial years. The initial years can be categorized as the first three to five years of marriage. Many can and will testify that these years may present themselves to be the hardest. I, personally, can attest that these years are definitely challenging, and they are not meant for the faint of heart. I repeat, "THEY ARE NOT FOR THE FAINT OF HEART." If I could, I would not only recommend premarital counseling, but I would recommend post-wedding counseling as well—especially during the initial years. Many acquire marital counseling as an intervention (once things are rocky), but I would like to suggest it as a preventative measure (while you are still good on the cliffs). One might ask, "Why get counseling when nothing is wrong?" That is a great question! In my experience as a pastor and as a husband, I have noticed a common theme throughout most, if not all, marriages. The common theme is that problems will arise. They are inevitable. After talking with many couples throughout the years, I've discovered that a lot of us are simply not equipped to handle the early challenges of marriage.

Note: I have not read nor heard about any such thing as what I call "preventative" Post-wedding counseling. While writing this book, I wanted to give you and other readers what I thought would have helped me, and the church members I've counseled, become more equipped to conquer the problems that plague new marriages. In my opinion, preventative post-wedding counseling should consist of couple's therapy and retreats that will allow you and your spouse to interact with other couples and also allow private time between you and your boo. One interesting piece of equipment is the bulletproof vest. This type of vest is designed to disperse the ammunition's energy and deform the round to reduce blunt force trauma. In other words, it is designed to lessen the blow of bullets. I would like you to think of preventative post-wedding counseling as a bulletproof vest for the marriage. It will not stop problems from hitting the marriage, but if done properly, it should lessen the blow of the problems. The whole breakdown or blueprint of what post-wedding counseling looks like will not be described in this book. That is another resource that I will offer in the near future. However, the point of bringing up such a thing is to encourage you to seek some form of prevention therapy in the early years of your marriage, to help you and your spouse become more equipped to handle the early challenges of your new life together. I have mentioned early challenges a few times now. Let us talk about what some of those early challenges may look like.

Imagine how you were raised. Next, imagine where you were raised. Lastly, imagine whom you were raised by. These thoughts may take you back to the family home, the street itself, the school district, the discipline you received, the strictness of your father, the tender love of your mother, the fights with your siblings, and so forth. Be it understood that your spouse had a totally different upbringing experience—not necessarily worse or better— just different.

However, you two may argue about who had the better upbringing. At this point, let's just focus on them being different and how conflict arises out of differences. With your spouse having a different background than you, he or she will not always view things the same as you. Make no mistake about it. You saw the very best of your partner during the dating stages. On the flip side, your partner saw the very best of you. This is common in many relationships because the idea is to win over the one we are courting. Many do not deliberately hide who they are. Many of us just focus on showing our strengths during our dating seasons, and because limited time is shared with one another, all sides will not be seen—or at least seen as much. So, we innately suppress in order to impress. Ooh, I like that! I think that'll preach!

If we are going to be honest, you probably did not know who you really were until you realized how different your spouse was from you. You had some dislikes before your marriage, but I am certain that you may have some newfound ones now. Believe me, I chuckled as I said that because I developed some pet peeves once married, and my wife for sure did too. Understand that being a perfect match does not mean that you are perfectly similar. YOU ARE DIFFERENT! I'll say it again, "Conflict arises out of differences." In the initial years of marriage, usually, the couple does not know how different they are from one another. The honeymoon experience will give you a false perception of what marriage will look like. It will give you a false perception of your partner as well. Do not get me wrong. It is your partner but only a fraction of them. You will really see each other as you really are when you began to do life together under one roof. Many of us who struggle early on in our marriages may say that our spouses are not who we thought they were. For some of us, I'd like to say yes, they were! It was just that they had other sides or possessed other characteristics that we did not notice during dating. However, to the rest of us, it is very well possible for us to have been hoodwinked. This book may not be useful for the latter group, being that the deceiver may not desire to contribute to a happy and healthy marriage. If both parties want to have a successful marriage, then both should be willing to be patient with each other—especially in the initial years.

Patience is key. Along with other key virtues that I will list in this book, patience will lessen the stress, arguments, fights, and resentments. Patience is not ignoring. In this sense, it is simply tolerating something that your significant other is doing that you wish they wouldn't. While tolerating the action, be optimistic about their growth. I am in no way telling you to be patient in abuse (physical, verbal, emotional, etc.), but be patient with your partner in the areas where they could just be lacking maturity. Be mindful that you lack full maturity in areas as well. As you tell your partner what you dislike about them, be sure to listen when they express their dislikes about you.

The purpose of this chapter is to help you understand that it is common for conflict to arise when two people have to adjust to becoming one. I did not do that well in my initial years of marriage. For example, I did not know how to let my singleness go. I am not talking about individuality. It does not matter how long you are married. You both will still have individuality. However, you will no longer be single. Don't get me wrong, I knew that I was no longer single, but I struggled with letting my single nature go. I would keep in touch with females that I knew before my wife. The keeping in touch itself was not the issue. It was the way I kept in contact. I did it secretly, and to be honest, I don't even know why, because I wasn't trying to rekindle anything. If you have to hide a friendship or relationship from your spouse, you should reconsider entertaining that relationship, because if your spouse finds out, it may not end well. If you find yourself doing this, ask yourself two questions: 1.) Why do you have to hide? 2.) What if your spouse was secretly entertaining a friendship or relationship? Believe me when I say this, it does not matter how old your secret is to you, once your partner discovers it, it will create a fresh wound and will not be easily bandaged. We will talk more about this in the chapter about infidelity. You should want to present a sense of truth and loyalty at all times. It is important to start out with these virtues and to maintain them throughout the marriage. Once they are tainted, you will catch hell trying to regain them.

So, I did not know how to let go because I was accustomed to having those relationships. I remember asking a woman during my first year of marriage, "Do you miss me?" My wife saw the text message and went berserk! She was furious! She said, "Dameon, you are a married man. You have no business asking another woman if she misses you." I heard her loud and clear, and to be honest, she was right. As wise as I thought I was at that time, I was acting out of immaturity. Mind you that prior to getting married, I was single for eight years. My last relationship before marriage ended when I was 19 years old. I really didn't have a serious adult dating experience until I met my wife when I was 27. I was inexperienced in a lot of areas. Yes, I could provide, protect, clean, and lead, but I shortly realized that I could not properly show her the attention, affection, and adoration that she needed. Also, there were things that I needed that she couldn't properly give at that time. Coming up short in those areas created tension for us. Just as we did not know how to manage our early challenges well, you and your spouse may find yourselves in a similar situation. If not combated properly, this type of mismanagement can occur years throughout your marriage. I assure you that the effects of such mismanagement can be catastrophic. I'd like to plead with you to expect certain immaturities and to alleviate them early on.

Both of you have the responsibility to acknowledge the person in the mirror. Both of you are responsible for dealing with the contents of your own bags. We all have some type of baggage that we bring to the marriage. Do not shy away from your bag! We are the way we are because of past experiences. Whether these are experiences of triumph or trauma, they have a hand in shaping our philosophies and personalities. Although you two may have experienced similar things, you will not have the exact life experience. Therefore, do not expect for your mate to view things the same as you. Don't get upset because they don't initially get excited by everything that excites you or get frustrated by what frustrates you. In time, they will learn what is of value to you and learn how to celebrate what you celebrate and be empathetic towards the things that you are sensitive about. Always keep in mind that you are a product of your experiences, and your spouse is not. He or she is a product of his or her own life's experiences. The sooner we realize this, the sooner we can begin to get over the hump (the major obstacle) that keeps us from progressing as a couple in the initial years.

Let us talk about these bags some more. These bags are nothing more than invisible collections of trauma, disappointments, loss, and other negative things that have the capability to weigh us down. If you are not careful, your baggage will present a burden to your marriage. It is very important to deal with the contents of your bag before the wedding. However, this is not always done because we may not be aware that we even have a "bag." I assure you that WE ALL HAVE A BAG! Some people take their baggage into the marriage and that same baggage will lead them into a divorce. Don't be like these people. Handle your sack! Once you begin to deal with your bag, you should come to realize that some issues you have are not your partner's fault. Proper blame placement is vital during the initial years, because you can jeopardize some potentially good years by treating your spouse as the "bad guy," when in fact, they were not the cause of your dissatisfaction. Now, it is possible for them to trigger a frustration of yours. But is that really their problem? Of course not! Usually, your spouse does not know of all your triggers. How can they know when, quite frankly, you don't? That is why you should explore and deal with your baggage prior to marriage. You need to know what triggers you and why. You need to know why you have these collections in the first place. Now, you do not have to explore your bag on your own. Some people have experienced more trauma than others and will need professional assistance. If you need professional help, please seek it. Typically, some form of therapy is worth the investment. Understand that your bag can affect every area of your life. It can have an effect on how you parent, work, socialize, and definitely on how you treat your spouse. Please do not allow your bag to be the reason that your marriage or any other area of your life fails. Take the time to understand why you are like you are—meaning why you think like you do and why you have the anxieties that you have, and so on. It will be hard for you two to become one if you do not know yourself.

My wife and I were accustomed to doing and not doing certain things before we met one another, and you and your spouse are no different. Depending on the length of time that you two spent dating, you probably had the opportunity to see your spouse's strengths and areas where improvements were needed. Generally, you may not see many areas where improvements are needed when the dating time is short. However, you will see those areas in the initial years. In the initial years of marriage (if you have not done so while dating), seek to find out your partner's love language, work ethic, aspirations, gifts, talents, likes, dislikes, passions, and hobbies. Find out what motivates them and try to identify what discourages them. In other words, learn all you can about the woman or the man that you love. Let me add that as you and your spouse get older, some things will change, and not just physical things. You may see certain aspects of life differently, as your many different experiences present new lenses for you to look through.

Initially, don't get hung up on the minute things. One may not clean as much. One may not cook as well. One may not be able to do laundry well. One may be a little more careless with money. One may have a difficult time expressing their feelings. One may drink or smoke too much. One may eat too much or too little. One may be absent from the home too much. One may be too much of a homebody. One may snore while sleeping. Or one just may have OCD. The point is that each of you will have some kind of "thing," but do not allow that thing to prevent you two from cherishing one another. Small things will only hinder you if you let them. Many couples that I have talked to made the mistake of not building each other up during the initial years of their marriage. Instead, they frequently pointed out the minute things, and all that did was beat insecurities and doubt into each other's mind. It was a hurtful thing to me, in our sixth year of marriage, to hear my wife repeat to me a statement that I said to her during our first year of marriage. Because I was not mindful of my words, I regrettably offended her. Although it was unintentional on my behalf, it was unforgettable on hers. I thought that being open and honest was noble, but what I was doing actually made me something that I would rather not say. However, my wife did give me the label. It rolled off her lips like she had been practicing it for weeks. Let's just say that it started with an "a" and ended with an "e" and no, it wasn't athlete. We have been married for a decade now. It was around the fifth or sixth year that I realized I could have done a lot of things differently, and I could have kept a lot of words to myself. I did a lot of damage that was not easily undone. Some things still require my attention to make right to this day. Take heed to just enjoy one another during those initial years. Love on each other as much as possible. Establish an unbreakable bond if it is not already present. Again, do not allow the little things to throw a monkey wrench in your happiness. Those minute things will work themselves out if you both are willing to work on them and be patient with one another.

Treat the initial years as the foundational years. Some may view the dating years as the foundational years; however, dating does not present the same reality as matrimony. Dating presents possibilities; marriage shows what has been made possible. While dating, the bank accounts are not combined, the last name is not changed, and usually there are two separate houses. In short, dating consists of two people being two, and marriage consists of two people being one. Marriage puts you into a very different and special category. Therefore, during the first years, the two of you should be laying the groundwork for the longevity of your marriage. Be intentional in combating the challenges that are known to plague the initial years of being married. With God on your side and you two working together, I believe y'all got this!

CHAPTER TWO:
Individuality

2

In chapter one, I mentioned how you should lose your singleness but not your individuality. Being single is a status while your individuality is your stamp. This stamp is your own individual uniqueness. As your status changes from being single to married, your stamp needs to further its presence into the world. Be careful not to lose YOU when you get married. You do not want your identity to be known just as so and so's wife or husband. You are "fearfully and wonderfully made," as Psalms 139:14a states. You are unique, and you were designed by the Almighty God to leave your mark in the world for His glory. This particular subject is needed because some individuals will be all they can for their spouse but will give nothing to the cause of being themselves. You can be one with your spouse and each of you can also have a signature. Issues are sure to arise when you can no longer be you or when your spouse can no longer be them. More often than not, women are mainly the ones to lose their individuality. This may be due to the dominance of men in most cultures. But there are some cases in which men have lost their individuality. Let's talk about how the tone is set for each to lose their individuality.

Let us deal with the ladies first. Many women will enter a marriage with the notion of being the best wife that they can be—as they should; however, they must understand that a woman can be more than just a wife. Not only should she understand that, but her husband should understand that as well. Let me put it this way. A woman can be a wife and a nurse. She can be a wife and a singer. She can be a wife and a comedian. She can be a wife and an Olympic gold medalist. You get my drift. In other words, she can have a calling outside of being just a wife. Let me tackle it from this angle. Michelle Obama is Barak Obama's wife, and Michelle Obama is *Michelle Obama!* She is an author, lawyer, Princeton and Harvard Law School graduate, and public servant. She has many accolades of her own, which has made her the "Forever First Lady" to some. She has individuality! Most women have dreams and goals before they get married. Do they disappear once they get hitched? Of course not, but if they are not careful, they will lose the motivation and desire to pursue those once golden ambitions. What we have deemed as gender roles in our culture may have set the tone for many women to lose their personal identities. Countless women have devoted themselves to those roles. They have mastered being mothers. They have mastered being wives. They have mastered cooking and cleaning. The question is, "Do they all master their aspirations?" After all, there is more to a woman's life than cleaning, cooking, bearing children, and homemaking. Right? Ask Michelle! So, women, it is okay for you to pursue those childhood dreams. Ideally, you should have discussed your future goals with your husband during the courting stage, and he should have discussed his with you. That conversation should have led to some form of planning for the two of you so that you both could be successful as individuals. I am well aware that you can have a conversation about these things and make plans only to find out that life doesn't always go according to your plans. You cannot control life. You have to make the best of it. Although life events can alter your plans, you should make every effort to resume what you had set out to do. Women throughout history have made essential contributions to society. Let that wonderful tradition continue with you.

As far as men go, we normally achieve our aspirations after the wedding. In some cases, we do not. Let's dive in and see why we don't. Every now and then, a man can end up with a very aggressive wife. Being aggressive is not necessarily a bad thing, but being too aggressive is definitely a hindrance to a happy, successful marriage. Most of the time, when the wife is too aggressive, the man can be forced to focus on her desires and needs and usually his desires will be put on the back burner. These types of men are labeled as weak men. Why? Because typically, men are the head or dominant ones in the relationship. Now, I will not brand them as weak men. Let me just say that maybe they are who they are because of what's in their bags. Maybe they saw their mom's or some other female caregiver's overly dominant nature and patterned themselves accordingly. If you are overly dominant, usually you will want everything to go your way. It's normally your way or no way. A woman like that is usually very contentious. The Bible warns men of such women. Proverbs 21:19 states, "It is better to dwell in the wilderness, than with a contentious and an angry woman." The wilderness is a place where a person is exposed to the elements of nature, the beasts of prey, and the want of necessities of life; however, this place is still better than to be where there is no peace and always a quarrel. Men who are in a situation such as this usually try to do whatever their wives say to keep them happy and their mouths closed. As a result, they find themselves without individuality. A man's life has more to it than just going to work, paying bills, fixing things, and making sure his woman is happy. Men, your stamp on life should supersede the corners of your property. There is greatness in you also, and hopefully your wives will see that and push you to excel in the dreams and goals that you have. Okay, if you are a handyman around the house, why not open your own handyman business? If you do a great job with your lawn, why not own a landscaping business? If you handle your finances and taxes well, why not be a tax advisor for the public? If you can teach your children algebra well, why not be a teacher at the local community college or university? My point is that you are gifted, and according to Proverbs 18:16, "A man's gifts maketh room for him, and bringeth him before great men." In other words, there is room for YOU outside of the rooms of your home. Be an excellent husband, but also pursue your individuality.

Now, let's not confuse individuality with selfishness. O.M.I.T. does not promote or condone actions that will jeopardize the sanctity of the marriage. Pursuing a profession that is not wholesome or morally sound can definitely cause problems. I do not recommend such ambitions. For example, a man saying that he'd like to leave his mark in the world by being a gigolo or a woman saying she'd like to be an escort is clearly beyond the realms of morality—especially as far as holy matrimony is concerned. Individuality is meant to add value to the marriage, not take away from it. I would like to shed light on some things that could suppress individuality from both male and female sides.

We saw where a woman could be too aggressive and cause her man to lose his uniqueness. History has also shown us that some men have also been too aggressive. According to the movie <u>What's Love Got to Do with It</u>, Ike Turner wanted Tina to do things his way all the time. She was to eat the cake when he said eat the cake. She was to sing songs the way he wanted them sung. When she did not do those things according to his liking, he resorted to violence to persuade her to do so. Tina's personal popularity superseded the popularity that she had with Ike simply because she fought for her individuality. She wanted the world to see who Tina was without Ike. Whether you are the husband or the wife, please do not try to control your spouse, because in doing so, you will create a breeding ground for misery and resentment.

> **"INDIVIDUALITY IS MEANT TO ADD VALUE TO THE MARRIAGE, NOT TAKE AWAY FROM IT."**

Another thing that can suppress the individuality of your partner is jealousy. In this sense, jealousy is you thinking that your spouse can't be for you outside of your sight. It's basically a thing of distrust. I get it! You married your spouse because he or she was attractive, talented, resourceful, and had a wonderful personality. However, it is not for us to dim the light of our significant other. They are called to be a light to the world and not just for your world. They have something to offer others, and we should be supportive of their individual goals and aspirations. Be careful not to be envious of them. It's nonsense to think that your spouse's success will overshadow your own. After all, your spouse is a reflection of you. If they look good, it will bring honor to your marriage as well. You should smile when your partner is successful. Not only should you smile, but you should think to yourself, "Look at my baby!" While thinking that to yourself, you should also encourage them to keep shining bright like a diamond.

Do not make the mistake of suffocating your spouse's dreams while trying to pursue your own. It's up to both of you to determine who should do what and when, when there is a "one at a time" situation. Finances, childcare, and education can all influence "who does what, when." I highly recommend that you both pray and allow the Lord to guide you with how the two of you move. Just because there is individuality does not mean that there's no team. There is nothing like a great duo. For example, Jordan and Pippen, Shaq and Kobe, Lebron and Kyrie, and

_____ and _____. I left those blanks for you to insert your name along with your spouse's name because you two are champions together. Think about it, you already have the rings!

The purpose of this chapter is to make you both aware of your status and your stamp. Remember, lose your single status, but keep your specific stamp. Encourage one another to pursue those dreams and aspirations. If possible, switch those stereotypical gender roles in order to give your other half the opportunity to maximize their potential. I have noticed in times past that since I was a pastor, people would only identify my wife as the preacher's wife. They would not allow her to be her own person. They would not allow her to make her own way. As a result, they put her in a box—per se. However, that is unfair to any individual. She does not live and breathe to be in my shadow. Instead, God has given her a path of her own to take while being a supportive wife to me. She had and still has different goals to pursue. I am finding myself more and more trying to be a help instead of a hindrance to her success. Men, it is imperative that you follow suit. If we are not careful, we as men will take the headship to the extreme. We should lead the household, but we should not hold back the house. You and your spouse should both excel at being individuals. This will help maximize your happiness and freedom together as a couple.

3   CHAPTER THREE:
In-Laws

T his chapter is designed to help you realize who you
married. You may marry into a family, but you do
not marry a family. Some individuals make the mistake of
not properly prioritizing the hierarchy of important individuals in their lives. I do not intend to downplay anyone's significance; however, I do intend to identify their
lanes. I came across a post on Facebook that had pictures
of certain females. It had a picture of a wife, mother, sister, daughter, and "baby mama." The caption read, "Rank
the order in which they should come." Obviously, this
post was to get the opinions of men. To my surprise, I saw
all types of opinions. Honestly speaking, all of our opinions should have been the same—at least the first three
should be the same across all classes of men. To give you
my opinion, to me, the wife comes first, then the daughter,
third the mom, fourth the sister, and lastly the baby mama.
All women have great significance, but each of them
comes with a certain level of priority.

What I am trying to illustrate here is that those under
your roof come first. Now, if you have children who are
not under your roof, they are still to be placed next to your
spouse in the order of priority. I've also read on social me-
dia where women have said that their children come before their spouse. Now, that rationale goes against the
natural order of the way God set up the household struc-

ture. Man is the head, then comes the wife, and thirdly the children. Biblical references to this order may be found in Colossians 3:18-21, Corinthians 11:3, and Ephesians 5:23. However, this chapter is not about the order in which children come (that should be a given); it is about the lanes of the in-laws. We'll talk about the order later.

Some in-laws or spouses' parents have a hard time releasing their authority over their children. I understand that their baby will always be their baby, but once that individual is an adult and married, that power cord is then cut. Do not get me wrong. The child's respect for his or her parents should always remain intact, but the parents should no longer exercise total control over their child. After the wedding ceremony, the couple will belong to each other. As Genesis 2:24 states, "Therefore shall a man leave his father and his mother, and shall cleave unto his wife: and they shall be one flesh." The "leave and cleave" principle here should be honored collectively by the newlyweds and their parents. The proper thought here for the parents should be that you are not losing a child, but you are gaining one. With that being said, just embrace the couple and try not to produce any conflict in their marriage. In a perfect world, this concept would be ideal, but since this world is not perfect...yep! You guessed it! Some parents will create conflict in their child's union. It is typical for some spouses to have a love/hate relationship with their in-laws. Now, I won't say too much about those relationships because my goal here is to get you, the couple, to not allow your in-laws to cause trouble between the two of you.

I am not fond of what I am about to tell you. I wish things would have happened differently. However, we cannot get any do-overs; so, I am stuck with this unfortunate story. In retrospect, I realize that growing up in survival mode created an awful character flaw within me. I was a very inconsiderate person when it came down to certain things. What I'm about to share with you now was an unfortunate act of inconsideration on my part. Okay, here goes. I married my wife before I was properly introduced to her father. I met her mom on my job prior to the wedding, but I never met her dad due to a conflict of schedules. We had scheduled to meet each other a couple of times, but he always called it off. I didn't know how to take that because to me he seemed uninterested. Being the independent fellow and alpha male that I was, I no longer cared to meet him. To understand my rationale, you would have to know what was in my bag at that time. See, the bag is always important. I was an orphaned child at the age of twelve years old. My mom died when I was two, and my dad died when I was twelve. I did not get to comprehend their married life at all. After my mom died, my siblings and I were split between different relatives. Every now and then my dad would try to regroup us, only for us to separate again. That was the cycle for a while. I stayed with a few relatives who had a husband and wife in the home. Two sets of the relatives consisted of aunts and uncles, and the other set consisted of grandparents. Unfortunately, none of the men took the time to teach me about life and what being a man consisted of. After my dad died, I basically had to figure it out on my own. From twelve years old and up, I just began to self-develop. I stayed with my grandparents, but being reared was a thing of the past. I did what I thought I was big and bad enough to do. I considered myself to be the black sheep of the house because of the unfair treatment that I received. I developed my own hustle to support myself at this very young age. I was a true hoodlum. From twelve to twenty years old, I ran the streets and was really not held accountable by anyone. When I was twenty, I changed my life around for the better. I was a churchgoing young man with an infant son. When I was twenty-one, I bought a house and continued to self-develop without any influence of a mentor or a father figure.

Now as I fast-forward to the time when I met Brittany, I was reputable, had my own home and a decent job, but I still had certain contents in my bag. So, when her dad kept blowing me off, I did what I was accustomed to doing. I just continued to be my independent self. Brittany and I dated for less than a year. I knew very quickly that I wanted her to be my wife. I asked her to marry me on Valentine's Day, and we got married two months later. Now here's the twist. I did not ask for her father's blessing. As a matter of fact, I didn't even know him. Wait! There's more! Her parents were out of town when we got married. That's the inconsideration on my part that I spoke of. I quickly got word from mutual acquaintances of ours that

Brittany's father was highly upset with me—and that's putting it in a nice way. From his standpoint, he had every right to be. His daughter was now married without him or his wife being in attendance, to a man that he had never met. I was sympathetic towards his point of view. However, he wasn't sympathetic towards mine. Shortly after Brittany and I were married, I finally met him. He did express his anger to me. Then I proceeded to tell him how I saw things. To make a long story short, I basically told him that I was unaware of a proper traditional protocol for these things. I had never seen a man ask a woman's father for his daughter. I have a sister. Although she had several boyfriends, no one ever asked to date her. There was technically no one to ask. In my defense, I had no clue about his prerequisites—especially since he kept calling off our meeting arrangements. All I knew was that I had found my wife and that I was ready to start a life with her. I wanted to hurry and get her out from under her apartment lease because I deemed it wise to stop spending that unnecessary money when I had a stable place for us to live. I was hoping that my father-in-law would have understood my position and written my actions off as acts of immaturity. I don't think he ever did. I even asked him to forgive me. I don't think he did that either. It's been ten years since our wedding, and he and I still don't have a solid relationship. We are not enemies, but we are not friends. I would occasionally get word that he was telling people that he didn't have a son-in-law. It was hurtful because it was just another form of rejection. Nonetheless, I was okay because at the end of the day, my priorities resided under my roof. I married her—not him.

I went down memory lane to set the tone for the rest of this chapter. Sometimes a series of unfortunate events will take place and leave you, the couple, with a dilemma. The dilemma usually calls for you to pick a side. I really hope that you will never have to choose between your spouse and your parents, but if this does occur, always choose your spouse because that's where your loyalty lies first. Be sensible about this piece of information, though. Don't choose your spouse if it is dangerous to do so. I now want to take the time to share with you how you should view your relatives while being married and how you should view your in-laws.

Let's deal with your side of the family first. I know that you love them and of course they love you. Family is everything. Right? Exactly! That's the point I am trying to make in this chapter. FAMILY IS EVERYTHING! When you said, "I do," you and your spouse became family. As a matter of fact, the family that you have created is the most important family. Why? Because you two are now the king and queen of your own castle. Wives, would you want your king to put another queen before you? Husbands, would you want your queen to put another king before you? I'm assuming that you both will answer, "No!" Therefore, treat your relatives well but not better than you treat your spouse. Putting your relatives before your spouse can cause bitterness in your mate. You've known your birth family your whole life, and they will always be your family, but once you get married, you have an obligation to solidify your new one. During the first couple of years of our marriage, Brittany would frequently visit her parents' home. This upset me so much! Don't get me wrong. I wasn't upset with her visiting them. I was upset with how much she was visiting them. Every time her parents would say they were cooking or having a cookout, Brittany had to be there. I remember telling her one time that she didn't have to go over to her parents' house every time they turned a burner on. I was trying to get her to see that she and I needed to bond more and solidify our new family. She and I both had sons prior to the marriage, and we had a son together during the first year. So, there was dad, mom, and three children. I felt like we weren't gelling as a family. I was working and pastoring at the time, so most of my time was spent on one of those clocks. It bothered me when I got free time because I had no family to spend it with. My family was usually at the in -laws' house. I didn't go with them often because I wasn't very comfortable. They were her relatives—not mine. Besides, my mind was on what was now my immediate family. I was pretty much a loner. I didn't have many friends, and my siblings and I were not as close as we should've been (this was due to us being separated most of our lives). I understand that me being a loner was not Brittany's fault. That was just the contents of my baggage. However, I did fault her for not properly prioritizing the people in her life. Now, I was not trying to control her. If that were the case, she would not have gone that much—at least not without some form of opposition. I wasn't, per se, a needy man, but I did need my wife to be MY WIFE. She had already spent years being a daughter, sister, and cousin, so I felt that she needed to get some "wife" under her belt. I married her because I wanted to share my life with her, but during that time, it seemed like we were not doing much sharing. It is imperative for you and your spouse to make sure you two spend a good quantity of quality time with one another—especially in the initial years. If your spouse voices to you that they feel like they're being placed on the back burner, please consider their feelings. It wouldn't hurt for you to examine your actions and make some adjustments in order to make your spouse feel like they are your priority. Don't make the mistake of winning over your lover during the courting season only to lose them after the wedding. What you did to get them is what it will take to keep them.

My wife didn't do much with her sisters, but she had a cousin that she considered to be a brother. Now, I mean, she was and still is crazy about this guy. When he would come to town, she made sure that she linked up with him. I honestly got tired of hearing his name. Mind you, I had nothing against him. I was just envious of the pedestal that she had him on. There was nothing wrong with her having him on a pedestal. He meant a great deal to her. I just didn't want him to mean more to her than I did. If you and your spouse are one, no one should come before your spouse or mean more to you than your spouse does. Your relatives will always be your relatives, and a good spouse will not try to keep you from them. Just be mindful not to make your spouse feel inferior to everyone else. That will only plant insecurities and create issues that may put your marriage in jeopardy. You may be wondering how I interacted with my blood family. Well, my interactions with them were very limited. I expressed to you earlier in this chapter that I was a loner. Therefore, my wife didn't have to worry about her in-laws being placed before her. I was more focused on trying to build the family I never had. The frustration came because it seemed like I was the only spouse trying to build the family. Your family needs an identity. It needs structure. Whatever that may look like, it's up to the king and queen to set the tone for their castle. It will be hard for you two to create your family's identity without spending the proper time with each other perfecting it. It's healthy for you to spend time with your relatives. It can also be refreshing, but just don't overdo it— especially at the expense of the happiness of your marriage.

Before I dive into my next point, I'd like to clarify that my wife did not intentionally put me on the back burner or try to make me feel inferior to her family. She was only doing what she was accustomed to. She grew up close-knitted to her family, and there was nothing wrong with that. She just didn't realize at the time that she had this brand-new family of HERS that needed to be solidified. She was young and inexperienced in this particular matter. I used to tell her often, "Baby, this is your house… be the woman of your house." I would say that because it was hard for her to be the woman of her house if she was hardly at her house. The purpose of Brittany's and my testimony is to let you know that it can happen without you knowing it. You may not intentionally desire to put your family before your spouse, and it may be already done once you realize it. The moral of the story is to make sure that you purposefully keep your relatives in the proper lane; then things will go more smoothly for you in your castle. Happy spouse, happy house!

Now, let's deal with your in-laws. They are very special people. Right? Of course they are. Appreciate them because your sweetheart came from their clan. While appreciating them, you have to remember that they are your spouse's blood and not yours. They may accept you and sometimes with biases. An issue may arise because you may not be used to this. I had a tendency of expecting the best out of people. I thought that the average person would possess the quality of being fair. Many can be fair, but can they be fair without prejudice? You may be thinking, "What does this have to do with anything?" And that's a good question. Usually, people want to be in good graces with their in-laws. If at all possible, we would love to be accepted by them. And there is nothing wrong with that because we are social creatures and have the innate need to belong. But sometimes the discrimination of the in -laws can discourage you. They discriminate by holding you to a certain standard, but they will be willing to excuse your spouse, who is their blood. Don't get me wrong. Your family may do the same on your behalf.

That's why your spouse may have certain feelings towards your people. Families have a tendency to back up family, no matter what. I'm sure you've heard the phrase, "Blood is thicker than water," which basically means that family comes before unrelated individuals. I'm not against that philosophy; however, I just don't think that you should back up bad behavior. Well, you shouldn't back up bad behavior unless you're an iniquitous individual. Now, let's say that when your in-laws present biases in situations that concern you and your spouse, it can cause you to question their integrity. If you are like me, a person's integrity will matter to you. Since your spouse's family is now your family, shouldn't they treat you like family? Well, that is ideal. However, that is not always the case. Say you go to your in-laws for support because your spouse is behaving in an unbecoming manner. Going to them is usually typical, because if anyone should be able to reach a person, it should be their family. Well, sometimes your spouse's family may opt out of calling them out on their misbehavior. This may cause you to feel like they are condoning your spouse's behavior. At this point, not only are you questioning their integrity, but you are also upset and may choose not to deal with them anymore.

Sadly, many spouses choose not to associate with their in-laws. Personally, I am a man of peace and I strive to "follow peace with all men," as Hebrews 12:14 teaches us. However, sometimes the best way to keep the peace is to avoid. You will not always see eye to eye with your in-laws. Therefore, going to them when you have a problem with your spouse will only make things worse for the two of you. Some people will tell you to keep what goes on in your house between you two and to not bring family into your business. That can be sound advice—especially if the other family members are known to be biased and unwise. It is key to remember that when you get the in-laws involved, they may not apply the "forgive and forget" rule. You and your spouse can make up and move on, but they may still hold that offense over your spouse's head. Believe me, that can create a very uncomfortable feeling for your spouse. It's a sad thing to not be able to call on family to help mediate issues be-

"IT IS NOT UP TO YOUR IN-LAWS TO DICTATE YOUR MARRIAGE, VALIDATE YOUR MARRIAGE, OR RESUSCITATE IT."

tween you and your partner. However, you must also remember that it is not their responsibility to intervene on your behalf. I get it! You may become desperate and reach out for help because you don't know of any other solution. Desperation caused me to reach out to my in-laws, and let's just say that I'd never do it again. If you and your spouse are going to work, then you and your spouse will have TO WORK. It is not up to your in-laws to dictate your marriage, validate your marriage, or resuscitate it. If there is a problem, you two should have a healthy conversation about it and resolve the issue quickly.

4   CHAPTER FOUR: Children/Parenting

Hopefully, the two of you want children. If not, please just scroll right along to the next chapter. If you two have decided to have a child or children, then there are some things that you both should be aware of. Whether or not to produce a child has caused issues in the lives of many married individuals. Children should be discussed thoroughly during the courting season because couples may have different outlooks on the subject. One may want children and the other may not. Your spouse should know where you stand on the subject. This chapter is designed to tell you how children can have an impact on your marriage. In addition to that, your different parenting styles could possibly clash as well.

Let me start off by saying that children are a joy! It's basically like seeing a reflection of yourself in human form—well, at least certain aspects of yourself. They will bring more meaning to your life and definitely more excitement. I know that mine do. The responsibility behind having children should help mold your life, but the children themselves should not control your life. Some people make the mistake of living for their child/children. You should always live for you. Just like I mentioned in chapter two about not losing YOU, don't lose you because of your child. Be there for your child. Be there for your spouse. Be there for you! Also, don't allow children to come between you and your significant other.

Now, I would say that you should have children only when you are ready for them. However, that's really not up to you. Being that God is the giver of life, He controls the how and the when. We can do the planned parenthood thing, but if God is not ready for us to conceive, it will not happen. It's always important to understand that things happen according to God's will and in His timing. If you two feel that you are not ready for children, take precaution and use preventative measures. Children come with great responsibility. They are wonderful balls of life that you will have the privilege of caring for. You will have to nurture, educate, and support them. They will need the both of you acting as a team to help develop them properly. You will be equally important in the development of your child. Do not just be present. Be active! If you are a father reading this, you should know that your involvement with your child can have more influence on them than you think. In my undergrad college years, I did a paper on when fathers are active in the lives of their child (ren). What I found through research was astonishing. I found that when fathers are active, daughters are less likely to experience teenage pregnancy, use drugs, or suffer depression. I also found that sons are less likely to join gangs, drop out of high school, or use drugs when their fathers are active in their lives. It's pretty much understood how much moms bring to the table. I must admit that there is nothing like a mother's love. I wasn't fortunate enough to witness my own mother's love due to her passing when I was two years old, but I have been a witness to seeing how so many mothers love their children. When both the loving mother and loving father are present and active, the child will more than likely develop well and reach his or her full potential—considering all things health-related being normal.

My wife thought it necessary for me to talk about the couple during pregnancy. There are some things that need to be understood when the woman is pregnant. We've had the pleasure of going through two pregnancies since we've been married. The first pregnancy happened during our first year of marriage, and the second is currently happening while I'm in the process of writing O.M.I.T. She would say that I am better during this pregnancy than I was during the first. I could vouch for the accuracy of such a statement if she decided to make it. You may want to know why I am better this go-around. Easy answer—when you learn better, you should do better. Down through the years, Brittany would tell me how I was putting so many things before her while she was pregnant. Mind you, I didn't mean to, nor was I aware of it. I was a young full-time pastor and a full-time employee. I was the founder of the church that I was pastoring at the time. I worked countless hours trying to build the church into a fully functional, relevant ministry. I was also working a lot of overtime hours at my secular job. Being busy with church and work caused me to allow my wife to go through this pregnancy pretty much alone. No woman should have to go through her pregnancy alone. The male responsible should be very much involved. Now, if you went to a sperm bank, my last sentence doesn't apply to you. As I was saying, I left Brittany to fend for herself many times during the first pregnancy, due to my being inexperienced. Fellas, making these mistakes can cost us later in our marriages. I'll deal with that more in an upcoming chapter. Basically, what we need to understand as men is that our wives are already considered vulnerable individuals when they are with child. Their health is compromised, hormones are all over the place, and the slightest thing may cause a miscarriage. Our job as men is to make their pregnancy as comfortable as we can. I had to learn this. If at all possible, if you can lift it, LIFT IT! If you can cook it, COOK IT! If you can clean it, CLEAN IT! The objective is to allow her to experience the least amount of stress possible when she's incubating the baby. I try to do more this go-around because I want to do all I can to ensure that she has a successful pregnancy. In addition to that, I do it because I have learned how to love her properly. Fellas, being a good father doesn't start when the child is born; it starts when the child is conceived. Be very helpful to your pregnant wife; and wives, be very patient with your husband—especially if he's inexperienced.

If you're not careful, children can drive a wedge between you and your spouse. It will not be the child's fault either. This usually happens because the couple shifts their focus to being parents so much that they stop being a couple. YOU CAN BE A COUPLE AND BE PARENTS AT THE SAME TIME. Don't allow the baby to come between you and your baby. I hope that didn't go over your head. There's enough love for everyone. As a matter of fact, there's a different love for everyone. Let me explain. According to the Greeks, there are multiple versions or different types of love. We have what they called Eros, Storge, Philios, and Agape types of love. Eros or Erotic love is a romantic, passionate type of love. Storge love is a type of love that you have for family. It's an innate love that you feel for your children, siblings, and other relatives. Philios or Philia love is a type of brotherly love. It's the type of love that you have for mankind. Agape love is the supreme love. It is unconditional and divine. It is how God loves us, and it is how we should ultimately love one another. With all of that being said, try to perfect your agape love for everyone, work on your storge love for your children, definitely make sure you have philia love for humanity, but whatever you do, please don't lose the erotic love for your spouse. May I add that "much spice will keep it nice." Couples sometimes will exemplify agape but will slack in the area of eros. It may not be intentional, but it is easy to let happen. Parenting, along with other roles that you may have to play, might cause you to experience stress overload, which in turn may cause fatigue. Let me promote self-care and rest because those are essential. But let me also suggest that making

> **"YOU CAN BE A COUPLE AND BE PARENTS AT THE SAME TIME."**

time for romance with your spouse is important as well. Women, don't spend so much time being a mother that you fail to be a wife. Men, don't neglect your husbandly duties while being a father. Always keep in mind that you two are top priority. Be willing to talk to your spouse if you feel neglected because he or she may only be focused on the child. If you are the one neglecting the other, remember that you vowed to put no one before your spouse. Always remember that God is to be first, then your spouse, and then your children. The point is that all have their respective places. DON'T NEGLECT ONE!

The previous paragraphs may have you thinking that I'm only referring to the couple and their biological child (ren). However, I was talking about all categories of children. For the sake of clarity, I would like to talk about certain issues that can arise in your marriage when there are stepchildren involved. This is definitely a conversation to be had. In my experience, I have seen where stepchildren caused conflict between couples. Now, for starters, I would like to say that you shouldn't look at the child as a "step" child. Look at him or her like your own, and you will treat them like your own. That's just general information that I want to share, but the real spill is how you two, the couple, deal with each other when a stepchild is present.

A problem can occur when the biological parent goes the extra mile to make their child feel wanted, welcomed, and needed in a blended family situation. There's nothing wrong with going the extra mile in and of itself. The problem arises when the child receives all the energy and attention, while the other spouse gets neglected. Just because the child was there first, does not mean that he or she should take precedence over your spouse. This could cause your spouse to be insecure, jealous, and angry. If your spouse is made to feel these things, it could have an impact on how they deal with your child. It is sad to say, but many children are abused and neglected because the stepparents are envious of their stepchildren. The marriage or family can't be successful where there is abuse and/or neglect. To lessen the chances of those types of negative feelings in your spouse, make every effort to have the proper hierarchy in your home. Now, some people will abuse or neglect children no matter what. That will not be your fault. That will be their own moral issue. I definitely pray that your home will not suffer any abuse or neglect of any kind. Remember that the both of you can seamlessly love the child together and still love each other as you should.

We've seen how issues can arise because of children. Let's explore how different parenting styles can clash in the home and make it difficult for the couple to get along. Hopefully, the two of you talked about your views on parenting before the child came along or the marriage began. It is to be understood that there is more than one method of parenting. I just suggest that you "bring them up in the nurture and admonition of the Lord" (Ephesians 6:4b). It's important to teach them about God and biblical principles so that they may grow up with the fear of the Lord in them, and be productive citizens of the kingdom of God and the society in which they live. Do you see how I feel children should be raised? Other people may think differently. Your spouse may have different views than you as well. Say you wanted your children to be raised in church and your partner didn't. That would cause friction. Say you believed in corporal punishment as a form of discipline and your partner didn't. You best believe that will cause friction as well. Say you want to teach your children hard life lessons when they make mistakes, and your spouse feels like that method is too extreme. You guessed it! That will also cause tension between the two of you.

The thing is that people have the tendency to model their parenting style after the parenting style they received as a child. Because you will have two different upbringings, you will have two different ideologies concerning parenting. The goal is to work together to determine what methods work best for your children. Also, understand that times change. Some techniques may have been useful during the era that you were being reared and not so effective now. Be wise in which practices you bring over because some may hurt more than help your child. All in all, just know that you are not raising you. You are raising a whole different human being. Work together and try to support each other's decisions as much as possible. Do not question what your spouse does in front of your child. This will more than likely show the child a weakness between the two of you that they'll exploit when given the opportunity. If you do have questions concerning something your spouse did, speak with them in a private setting away from the child. I have learned that this is the smartest and more mature thing to do. It'll make your spouse feel like you guys are more of a team and not just a couple that's parenting individually.

Again, please be mindful to keep your spouse in his or her proper lane. I'm not saying that your spouse is greater than your child or that your child is greater than your spouse. I'm just saying that when you're prioritizing your allegiance, your spouse should come first. Children will one day leave the nest and start families of their own. Don't make the mistake of losing each other because your household has gained another individual. Continue to date, explore, and cherish one another, and definitely keep that EROS flowing.

CHAPTER FIVE: 5
Finances

I have seen where couples have kept their marriages free of infidelity, abuse, and neglect but allowed their mismanagement of finances to ruin their union. As with anything involving marriage, the key to success is the partnership. I hope that you watched very carefully how your spouse dealt with his or her finances while you were dating. You could then have an idea whether they were wasteful or wise with money. Problems can occur in your marriage if one of you wants to spend too much or too little. Usually, the breadwinner will want to establish their dominance over the financial direction of the family. Traditionally, the breadwinner was the man, but women are becoming the breadwinners in modern times due to their education and the career fields they've chosen. The glass ceiling is also becoming a thing of the past, which is making it possible for women to bring more money into the home. However, it does not matter who the breadwinner is. The financial goal between the two of you should be to sustain the family's way of living. No one should put their family's wellbeing in jeopardy because of money mismanagement. If one of you has a problem with managing money, please take some money management courses. Usually, your local bank will offer these courses or seminars for free.

I am no financial planner or advisor. I have the "el cheapo" label attached to me from my closest friends and acquaintances. However, I'd like to say that I'm just very conservative and not cheap. I can spend big if I need to, or I can save if I need to. At the end of the day, I want to have something to show for the money I've spent. Now, Brittany has other characteristics when it comes down to spending money. She likes to buy what she needs and wants. The thing with her is that she'll spend without a budget and usually will have the very minimal amount to show for it. Because we both have learned this about ourselves, we've learned how to communicate heavily in this area to make sure we put our money to good use.

You should know your partner's spending habits. You should also know yours. Be honest with yourself if you are hindering the progression of your financial status. It has come to my attention that everyone did not learn to balance and budget. If this is you, don't beat yourself up over it. Just yield yourself to be educated on those things now. If your partner is better at handling money than you, allow him or her to lead in that area to ensure your home's financial stability and success. Just make sure you know what's going on.

The most frequent issue that I've seen is where a spouse has the means to help the other spouse financially but won't. You may find this strange, or this may describe you in some way. The scenario behind this point lies with a couple who came into the marriage with separate debts and have not opted to combine their monies yet. Maybe there were car notes, student loans, or credit card balances before the wedding. Some couples will continue to pay their separate bills. There's nothing wrong with that if you have that understanding and can remain in harmony with one another. Whether or not you combine your bills and monies is totally up to you. At the end of the day, you have to do what's best for you and your house. I strongly believe that if you and your spouse continue to pay your bills separately, one should be willing to help the other if he or she comes up short—especially if the means are there to do so. If your spouse is careless with their money because they know that you will bail them out, then that's a different situation. I can understand your reluctance to help if that is the case. The only advice I can give on that is that you pray and also seek professional couple's counseling. Hopefully through counseling, someone can mediate and cause your prodigal spouse to see the stress they're causing.

Back to the initial point that I was making. If your spouse is wise with their money and happens to have a "ways off" pay period and can't meet their financial obligations, as a spouse, you should be obliged to come through for them. To watch your partner struggle, knowing you can help, can jeopardize your relationship. It will make your spouse question your commitment to them and your love for them. Furthermore, struggling can add stress to an individual. Stress produces vulnerability and the need to vent. It could very well be another issue if your spouse vents to the wrong person. "Who is the wrong person?" you may ask. Good question! The wrong person is the one to play on your spouse's vulnerability and provide for them what you are not willing to provide. Usually, when they provide that something, they will be expecting something in return. Now, that's not always the case, but I've seen it happen many times. Bottom line is that if you can help your spouse financially, do it. If possible, work together to alleviate the debt that you both have. All it takes is careful planning and commitment.

Some have asked me for my opinion on couples sharing bank accounts. What works for me and my house may not work for every household. I entertain the possibility of having at least three bank accounts. A personal account for each of the spouses and a joint account shared by them both. The personal accounts should be used for personal desires. For example, a new watch, a new dress, a new phone—basically what you can afford to buy. The joint account should be used to take care of the household or living expenses. For example, the mortgage, utilities, car note payments, toiletries, etc. Both parties should contribute to the joint account whatever amount they decide in order to ensure sufficient funds. Each should be responsible for what goes in and out of their own personal accounts. And of course, it's okay to contribute to your significant other's personal account. It is okay to also have independent or shared saving accounts in addition to the ones I've already mentioned. You can't have too much money. Right? I don't think so.

The point of this chapter is to get you to see that you should have a working plan when it comes to your finances. Don't allow money to come between you and your spouse's happiness. I've seen couples with less money who were happy-go-lucky. I have also seen couples with a nice, shared income, but because they lacked partnership, their marriage was always full of tension. Make sure you choose a good narrative for your finances. I also recommend that you don't think money is everything. Don't spend so much time trying to make a living that you don't live. Enjoy one another on a small budget just as you would on a larger one.

6 CHAPTER SIX: Spirituality

I do preach and teach that we are spiritual beings housed in a physical body during our tenure here on Earth. The book of Galatians in the Holy Bible admonishes us to live and walk in the Spirit. Therefore, it is necessary to discuss marriage and spirituality because problems can arise in marriages when partners are not on the same page spiritually. Maybe you were raised to believe in different faiths. I personally believe that there is only one true Lord, one faith, and one baptism as Ephesians 4:5 states. However, I also recognize that there are many other practiced religions in the world. Just as there are many other religions, some people will find love with a person of a different faith than they have. Now, I am not totally sure how you can find common ground in this type of situation, because your faith should shape your values, character, and behavior. I am not saying that the two can't love each other. I just find it difficult to see them being devoted to their different faiths without them clashing with each other in some form or another.

The purpose of this chapter is to help the couple become more understanding towards one another where there is a disproportionate amount of spirituality between the two. Depending upon where and how you were raised, spirituality may or may not be a big factor in your life. But for some, the question is, "What should you do when your spouse isn't as spiritual as you desire them to be?" This is a real problem for some; I have witnessed it on a few occasions. Before I go any further, let's talk about what it means to be spiritual. Being spiritual consists of believing that there is a power higher than yourself. It is believing that this power is supreme and is in control of all forces. This power connects us to nature, humanity, and all things seen and unseen. It also consists of believing that everything happens for a reason and that we as humans are created by this higher power (God) to carry out individual life purposes. In some cases, it means to be religious as well. With all that being said, some are more serious about being spiritual than others. Due to the levels of spirituality between the couple being unbalanced, sometimes a strain will be placed on the marriage. Strain is nothing but stress, and stress can be the silent killer for anything. So, in order to avoid this stress, couples should make sure that they understand each other's stance on spirituality and/or religion.

It is not uncommon for couples to have different perspectives on their spirituality. It is wise to discuss these differences during the dating phase, so you will know if the differences are enough to be deal breakers or whether they can be compromised. I have seen times where individuals complained about the lack of spirituality shown by their partner. More often than not, it was normally women who were complaining about the men they were dating or married to. Usually, in today's time, men are less likely to be spiritual or religious beings than women. Also, many women are hopeful in thinking that the man will change (do better as far as this subject goes) after they get married. There's nothing wrong with being optimistic, but you should be willing to be patient because this usually doesn't happen overnight. Depending on how serious this matter is to you, be hesitant to marry if you feel you are spiritually unequally yoked. Going forward with matrimony in this type of situation will more than likely cause resentment and regret.

It is also possible for both involved in the relationship to not be spiritual at all at first, and then, at some point during the marriage, one may be converted to a certain religion. This type of situation can also be frustrating to both individuals. The converted spouse may be frustrated because their significant other will not convert, and the unconverted spouse may be frustrated because his or her partner has changed and is trying to force their newfound faith on them as well. With this type of scenario, both should be understanding of each other's position. Be careful not to waste valuable time quarrelling over something that just needs patience to work through. The converted should be patient with the unconverted, and the unconverted needs to be patient with the converted. The converted must realize that with any newfound faith, it will take time for them to develop and mature in it. The best way to try and convert your partner is to represent your faith well by living it out before them. Pressuring them with harsh words will only push them away from wanting to participate. The unconverted should realize that with new practices, some errors are bound to happen. There-fore, he or she should be understanding and supportive in his or her spouse's attempt to live this new life. Note: if this newfound faith is an occult or satanic practice, I do not recommend that it be supported. That's just me, though; but to each its own.

If you feel that your spouse's religion is noble and is helping them to become a better person, try not to hinder them by downplaying what they are doing. The last thing you want is for your partner to feel unsupported and criti-cized by you. Be understanding and patient because usu-ally, people will find purpose in life through their faith. So, your spouse could be finding themselves more and more as they study the doctrine of their religion. Allow them time to grow in it, or the time to realize that it's really not for them. Either way, let it be their choice. If you are of a different conviction than your spouse, I hope that the two of you will learn how to agree to disagree. Make no mistake about it, this type of situation may pose some challenges. Some faiths may clash with one another but remember that you married the individual and not their faith. I say this because you may find yourself hating what they believe in more than you find yourself loving on them. Take heed not to make your spouse feel alone on their newfound journey. This could open the door for an-other person to fill the void of validation and support. I'm not saying that acts of infidelity will be committed be-cause of this. However, I am saying that you should do all that's in your power and within reason to make sure your spouse never needs anyone else to do what you can do for them. This can be dangerous for your marriage because your spouse may find themselves being dependent upon someone else, and the dependency can lead to an attraction. In some cases, these attractions may lead to attachments. These attachments may lead to "entanglements." It's pretty much understood that what you won't do, another will. Do not give another person the opportunity to have an inappropriate attachment with your spouse. Be mindful that some will try it through religion.

Now, if you are the one with the new faith, you should be patient and understanding as well. Not all changes are smooth. Your spouse may need time to adjust to your new practices. Remember that they met you one way, and now you may be changing tremendously. Sometimes, your spouse may feel that you're taking them too fast. This usually happens because you may change quickly and drastically. I'm not saying you shouldn't progress quickly in your endeavors. I'm just encouraging you to be mindful of how your partner may be processing everything. For instance, say your religion calls for you to change your diet and dress, or attend multiple gatherings weekly, or obligate you to pay a nice sum of money often—these new practices can very well affect your spouse. Therefore, listen to them and be considerate of their feelings if they voice their concerns or complaints. It may not be that they want you to stop; they may just want to be assured or reassured that your practices won't jeopardize the family in any way. Most people's ideologies are shaped by their faith. If your way of thinking is different now because of your new religion, think about how your spouse may feel—considering that you may have had a different thought process before. It may take a little while for them to get adjusted to the new you. In some cases, if spouses think the change is too extreme, they may never get adjusted and could possibly want out of the union. I pray that this will not be your case, but just be mindful that this can be a possibility.

If you two are not spiritual and are searching for a faith, may I suggest Christianity. Sure, there are some who may find fault with the Christian church, but honestly, you can find fault with any religion if you look for it. I recommend Christianity because it has worked and is working for me on a personal level. I also recommend it because it is the great commission to compel people to Christ. Marriage is the first institution ordained in the Christian bible, and because of its principles, my marriage has weathered many storms. The Bible can help a man be a better husband and a woman to be a better wife. In return, it can help a husband be a better man and a wife to be a better woman. It teaches on faith, forgiveness, love, wisdom, sacrifices, money, obedience, disobedience, sin, evil, blessings, curses, afterlife, and so much more. Every aspect of life is touched on in the Bible to some degree, leaving the believer with hope and assurance of leading a well-balanced and prosperous life. You may want to know why I chose to follow Jesus. Well, I chose Him because He first chose me. Being spiritual means that you're able to communicate with your creator, and He can also com-municate with you. I was visited very early in life by the spirit of the Lord, and He revealed His purpose for me and my life. Although I didn't accept His call right away, I did accept it when I was a young adult. I must say that choos-ing Christ was the best and most important decision that I have ever made, and the second most important decision was choosing Brittany to be my wife. Best believe that the first decision helped tremendously with the second. When I thought about giving up on my marriage, prayer and re-lying on God's Word helped me to hang in there and fight harder for my family. Understand that sometimes your faith will do what your money, education, social status, or relatives can't. That's why it is important for you to trust in something higher than yourself. Being that we are peo-ple, we are subject to err, but there is no failing in God. He made us, and He designed marriage; therefore, He knows how to help us have a prosperous life and success-ful marriage.

Just in case you don't know of any biblical teachings concerning marriage, let me share a few with you. The Bible teaches men to love their wives as Jesus Christ loves the church. Christ loved the church so much that he died in one of the most gruesome ways an individual can be killed. The application here is to see it as a man being self-less and a protector for the woman he wedded. He should honor her, adore her, and cherish her. The Bible also teaches that wives should submit to their own husbands. This scripture is usually taken out of context by both women and men. Some feel that this gives off a type of dictator-like or bossiness vibe. What the Bible teaches here is the structural hierarchy of the household. It's to be understood as this: God is the head of the man, the man is the head of the woman, and the woman is the head of the children (I will write more about this in Chapter 9). With any type of headship position, the subordinates should be obedient to their respective heads. So, submissive here means to be obedient by allowing the husband to lead the household as he receives his direction from his head (God). The fifth chapter of Ephesians is concluded by Paul exhorting the man to love his wife as he loves himself. When a man loves himself, he will nourish and cherish himself. He will make sure that he has everything he needs. Therefore, if the man loves his wife as himself, he will do likewise for her. Paul is also encouraging the woman to revere her husband. This means to honor and respect him. Appreciate and speak highly to and of him. It's befitting for Paul to address these areas, being that women thrive more off attention and affection and men thrive more off respect and honor. Biblical principles are in fact great sources to help couples with their spirituality. To get more information about the Christian faith, find a good Bible-based church where the leaders teach and practice God's unadulterated Word.

7 CHAPTER SEVEN: Surviving Infidelity

I pray that you will never have to experience infidelity in your marriage, but if you do, you need to know that you can overcome it. However, be it known that this type of situation is never easy to get over. You will not be able to do it on your own. You will need God, prayer, much cooperation from your partner, and the ability to exemplify forgiveness. In some cases, you may need professional help (therapy) as well. If you are the adulterer, please know that your partner will need these things, and you should not expect them to heal or "get over it" overnight.

The terms adultery and infidelity are usually used interchangeably. Adultery itself is defined as one having sexual intercourse with someone other than his or her spouse. Infidelity is basically when there is unfaithfulness in the marriage. You can have infidelity without adultery, but you can't have adultery without infidelity. It is one of the most hurtful things that can happen during matrimony. Some individuals can never shake this type of action and may want a divorce. Biblically speaking, they will have a sound reason to back their position. As Jesus states in Matthew 5:31-32, "It has been said, Whosoever shall put away his wife, let him give her a writing of divorcement: But I say unto you, That whosoever shall put away his wife, saving for the cause of fornication [adultery], causeth her to commit adultery…" According to that scripture and the law of marriage, I teach that only adultery and death are biblical grounds to dismiss one from marriage. Although death is obviously an ender, adultery doesn't have to be. Some will choose to stay because their love for their spouse will outweigh the offense. That agape love that I spoke of earlier has the ability to cover a multitude of faults. If you are willing as a couple, you can overcome infidelity.

Before I get into overcoming infidelity, please allow me space to talk of ways to try and prevent it. Now, you have to know that some partners will be greedy. They will

> "IF YOU ARE WILLING AS A COUPLE, YOU CAN OVERCOME INFIDELITY."

want what they have at home and more. In cases like that, you will have to acknowledge that they have a heart condition—and that condition is lust. They will need to be delivered from that. Maybe that should be a different topic for a different day or at least for a different book. However, I would like to illustrate ways to possibly prevent infidelity in marriages where there is no greed but there are loopholes. I call these loopholes cancers of marriage. If not checked, they will grow into something ugly and painful. Sometimes infidelity can begin in the form of little snowballs, and before you know it, they will be rolling downhill uncontrollably, full steam ahead. Now these snowballs or cancers usually derive from some form of neglect in the marriage. Maybe there's not enough attention, affection, sex, communication, support, or respect given to either one of the spouses, or they both may be falling short of providing these things to one another.

I have seen where one will reach out to the other and request such things, but to no avail; the partner doesn't respond, and things stay the same. After a while, after much pleading, the petitioner will develop a dissatisfaction (cancer). This displeasure with their spouse may lead them to be pleased by another.

Preventing this avalanche of snowballs from falling may just rest in your willingness and ability to stay on top of your spouse's needs—whether they are physical, mental, or emotional. Couples tend to make the mistake of going all out in the courting season and then easing up tremendously in the marriage. Remember, "what it took to get them, it's going to take to keep them." Hats off to you for you wooing your partner in the beginning, but you will have to woo them throughout the marriage. I saw in my own marriage how my wife and I failed to give each other what we needed. We were fine during our dating period, but things began to unravel when we started living together under one roof. She was more emotional, and I was more physical. In other words, she needed me to appeal to her emotionally, and I needed her to satisfy my physical desires. Don't get me wrong; we needed other areas tended to as well. These were just our dominant love languages at the time. We became distant because I didn't know how to properly show her the attention and emotional support that she needed (she required these things because of what was in her bag). Mind you, I loved her dearly, but I was inexperienced in this particular area. I grew up very naïve, and since I was always in survival mode, I never learned how to be there for a woman like that. On the other hand, I was a hard individual. An independent guy. I had learned to build myself up. I had no emotional issues—well, at least I thought I didn't. I assumed that I had decluttered my bag. All I felt I needed was for my woman to love and appreciate me. Now when I say "love," I mean in every sense of the word. I think that's where my issue came in. I wasn't being loved or loved on like I thought I should have been. I'm not trying to make excuses for either one of us or justify our actions. I'm just trying to explain to you how things can begin to go south if you are not careful. As you can see, I don't mind our story being a testament or proverb if it will keep you from making the same mistakes that we made as a young couple.

As I stated, in the initial years, try to learn as much as you can about your spouse. If you do this, you should successfully see the areas that they need the most affirmation in. Your spouse will more than likely always let you know what they need. Take heed to what they mention to you the most. Oh, how I wish that I had this O.M.I.T. tool when we first got married. Having a "heads up" sure would have made a world of difference. Okay! My rant is over.

I would like to speak on this matter to the one who broke the vows first. It is important to go this route first, because usually the one who breached the marriage covenant doesn't know to what extent they hurt the other spouse. Think about it for a moment. This individual trusted you so much, to the point where he or she decided to spend the rest of his or her life with you. With that also came them giving you their heart, trust, loyalty, and more. When they said, "I do," they had no idea that you would one day break their heart and cause their world to shatter. That type of hurt and disappointment has the capability of changing a person forever. Be careful before you say, "Deal with it" or "Let's move on." Those things are harder to get over for some than they are for others. People have different processing times and procedures. Maybe your spouse needs more time to process the act(s). Allow them the time they need without rushing them to get over the infidelity. At all costs, try to be sensitive and understanding about their requests. At some point, they may begin asking you questions about the affair. This happens because they're trying to figure out what went wrong or whether they are to blame. You may feel interrogated but sometimes it will not be interrogation. Cheating on your partner will oftentimes cause them to have insecurities and feel inferior to the person with whom you cheated. Therefore, those questions may be them trying to get a sense of what they are worth to you. Let me also add, sometimes it may just very well be interrogation. This may be because you're dealing with a scorned individual.

Hurt damages a person in ways the offender may never know unless they have worn those shoes before.

With that being said, please be understanding with your spouse. Bouncing back is doable, but it is never easy. They can become a mental wreck. Almost anything can trigger them into thinking about the infidelity. Triggers can be anything from, but not limited to, a certain song, building, beverage, person, or picture. If they are not careful, triggers can cause the wounds to reopen and the pain to resurface. They will need to learn how to cast down the need to react when they encounter something that will trigger them about the infidelity. In some cases, people will get to a point where they begin to ignore the things that trigger them. They will normally make a conscience choice on their own to do so. On the other hand, some people may need a professional to help them learn how to move past acts of infidelity.

"IT'S VERY IMPORTANT TO IDENTIFY THE ROOT CAUSE OF WHY YOU OR YOUR SPOUSE WANTED TO INDULGE IN ACTS OF INFIDELITY IN THE FIRST PLACE."

Let's talk about how to survive infidelity. It's very important to identify the root cause of why you or your spouse wanted to indulge in acts of infidelity in the first place. Like many, when you said your vows, you meant to honor them until death did you part. However, somewhere along the way something changed, causing you to renege on your promises. Usually, it's due to a lack of receiving something from your partner or marriage. That's why it is important to communicate and share often with one another to make sure that you two understand each other's position, needs, and desires. Be willing to listen to your spouse's plea and consider their needs. Once you have identified the void (root), begin to work in that area. If it was a lack of affection, intentionally be more affectionate. If it was a lack of romance, intentionally be more romantic. If it was a lack of support, intentionally be more supportive. Whatever your case may be, intentionally do better in the areas where you fell short. Make no mistake about it; I am not saying that you should take full responsibility or blame for your partner's infidelity because you failed to provide something. Your partner made a conscious decision to participate in those certain acts. Let me also add that I do recognize how vulnerability can cloud one's reason and influence unbecoming choices. With that being said, if you are the spouse who finds themselves in a vulnerable state often, it will be beneficial for you to find other ways to deal with your vulnerability instead of turning to infidelity. I know that may be challenging at times, but you'll feel accomplished knowing that you occupied yourself with something positive and constructive versus something painful and destructive. You will sleep better at night knowing that you kept up the integrity of your marriage even when it didn't seem favorable.

Keeping these things in mind, understand that it is going to take both of you to intentionally overcome infidelity.

CHAPTER EIGHT:
Dating, Sex, and Romance

8

There's no need for me to get super spiritual with this chapter. I do recommend that we observe the statutes of God concerning the subject, though. As the Bible states, "Marriage is honorable in the sight of the Lord, and the bed is undefiled." I love to say it like this: Before marriage, the bed is for sleeping; after marriage, the bed is for sexing and God is okay with that as long as it's with who you are married to. This chapter deals with things that are more on a physical and intimate level. Therefore, you must not be so spiritually minded on sex to where you are no good during the sex. Jesus says that there will be no marriages in Heaven. He states that everyone will be like the holy angels. With that information, we can conclude that sex is a temporary thing for this temporal Earth's institution of marriage. Therefore, enjoy it while it lasts!

Now let's talk more in-depth about sex and romance. Although sex and romance are often used interchangeably, they are actually two different things. Sex is the act of fulfilling the physical desire to climax sexually by way of oral and/or genital stimulation. Although not recommended, people can really find sex anywhere. Many pay for escort services, link up with old high school or college crushes, have sexual relationships with coworkers, etc.— all to achieve physical pleasure. While sex can be found in a variety of places without much effort, one must be intentional with bringing romance into his or her relationship. We'll talk about actual sexing later in the chapter. Let's deal with romance now. Romance is an art of expression—expressing your affection for your partner, that is. It is what you do before and after sex. Honestly, romance makes sex more passionate and intimate.

In my studies and observations, I've come to find that many husbands fall short in the area of wooing their spouse with quality romance. Notice that I mention the word "quality." That's because being romantic consists of providing quality time, quality gestures, and quality affirmations to your spouse.

"ROMANCE IS AN ART OF EXPRESSION— EXPRESSING YOUR AFFECTION FOR YOUR PARTNER, THAT IS."

Oftentimes, after the honeymoon season of the marriage, a lot of fellas are only concerned with the quantity of sex rather than the quality of romance. On the other hand, women are more geared to look for the quality of romance versus the quantity of sex. However, if the quality of romance is satisfactory for her, she will definitely increase the quantity of sex. A lot of men, including myself have been guilty of being romantic in the dating season, or in other words, the beginning of the relationship. Once we've satisfied the hunt, per se, and obtained the beautiful specimen that caught our eye, sometimes we make the mistake of becoming too relaxed, and we abandon the romantic gestures that we initially displayed in the courting process. It is the wooing that penetrates the woman's heart and causes her to fall for the one in pursuit of her. There-fore, continued wooing even after the wedding causes her to keep falling and remaining so much in love. It'll be hard for the guys on the job, in the street, or anywhere else to stand a chance with a wife whose husband is intentional with keeping the romance going in the relationship.

In our society, we are normally socialized to think that it's the man's job to be the romantic one in the rela-tionship. However, marriage is a partnership and requires both parties to equally contribute to the success of keeping the fire burning. So, women, while requiring your man to be more romantic, make sure you are romantically in-volved in the relationship as well. Many men may be similar to me. It doesn't take much to please an ol' coun-try boy like myself. Outside of peace and pleasure, I am very easy to satisfy. Nevertheless, I still appreciate my wife attempting to be romantic with me. I can remember times when I would pull out a notepad at work and would come across a paragraph that Brittany wrote on a random page. She would simply write things like, "I love you, baby," with some form of affirmation with it. What would make me smile the most was seeing her signature at the bottom of the letter with a heart above the "i" in her name. I could feel the love straight off the pages because she wrote from her heart. To her, that was intimate and affec-tionate (remember, her love language is showing affec-tion), and I was able to feel and appreciate it. She has packed me lunch before and placed a love letter with it. For my birthdays, she would set me up with spa days to receive pedicures and massages. She would make those days all about me, and it wasn't because she wanted anything in return. She just wanted me to feel her affection towards me. I appreciated it. If I can be honest, although I was grateful for her kindness, I failed to cherish it like I should've. I know, right? Shame on me. Fellas, please don't make the mistake of not properly cherishing your wife's efforts like I did. What you fail to cherish, you may cause to perish. Now that's a word, husbands and wives. So, if and when your wife does anything for you, whether it's fixing your plate, ironing your clothes, giving you a compliment, or writing you love letters, be appreciative and intentionally acknowledge her efforts. Think about it! What you appreciate lasts.

I can't close on the subject of being romantic without offering ways couples can be romantic with one another. Some things I mention may be gender-oriented or gender-neutral. It just depends on the individuals and their culture. One can be romantic by taking his or her spouse to certain places that will unlock feelings of bliss. These places may include: parks, beaches, movies, restaurants, concerts, and balls. While you are at these places, do adorable things that your partner will cherish forever. Plan many dates and picnics. If possible, try to go out on a date at least twice a month. I understand that having small children can hinder frequent dates, but try to find alternate ways to spend quality time with one another if babysitters are not available. Not too much can compare to spending quality time together. Good quality time is essential to a long-lasting, healthy relationship. Cooking for your spouse can be considered a romantic gesture. Think about it, we normally eat for nourishment. So, you might ask, "When is cooking considered romantic?" A meal is considered a romantic gesture when it is not cooked just for nourishment but for enjoyment. How does this sound? "Baby, tonight is all about you. I'm making your favorite meal exactly how you like it. I'll have the table set with candles, and we'll drink your favorite wine." Now that's romantic. Fellas, if the kitchen isn't your forte, fire up that grill and create a steakhouse setting for your queen. She'll love the idea that you are standing over that grill with the intention of making something special just for her. In case you haven't noticed yet, women love to be spoiled. But make no mistake about it, they love to do the spoiling too. Another thing you can do is go on car rides together. Drive with no destination in mind. The purpose is not to go somewhere physically but somewhere intimately. Hold hands (if possible) and have meaningful conversations while cruising. My wife loves a good intimate drive.

In the event that cooking, seeing a movie at a theater, going to a restaurant, or some other thing that I have mentioned may be too expensive for you, try doing non-costly romantic things. Give each other compliments. Hug on each other and give passionate kisses on the forehead, lips, or neck area. Text or call each other here and there to let one another know that you are thinking about the other. Be goofy or witty with each other. I had to learn from my wife that being romantic and affectionate doesn't always have to cost something. A nice walk up the neighborhood street is romantic to her. Lying in bed cuddling while watching a movie also does it for her. Remember, being romantic is not about you. It's about making your special someone feel how special they are to you. If you listen and pay attention carefully, your spouse will give you the blueprint on what they deem to be romantic.

Now let's be adults for a little while. Well, nasty adults. Yes, I am laughing, but I am also very serious. Having sex is a serious thing when married, and it is a real vital part of a long-lasting healthy relationship as well. The lack of sex or the type of sex craved can lead to sexual frustration and has the tendency to open the door to infidelity. I included chapter seven to help couples survive infidelity. However, the goal is to prevent it. Some couples have no issues with their finances, communication, or parenting styles. On the other hand, the issue lies in the bedroom sometimes. Growing up, I used to think that men were the sex monsters. You know… always wanting it. As I got older and started to converse with more and more women, I came to find out that women crave sex just as much as men. And they just don't crave sex, they crave good, hot, passionate sex. Therefore, it is imperative for you and your spouse to be intentional in making time to pleasure one another sexually as often as necessary. As a car needs to be tuned up to function properly, so does your spouse. Change her oil, rotate his tires –whatever you call it, by all means, just do it. I've literally witnessed my wife's whole demeanor change after a good sexual healing. There have been times where I've been rowdy and after she worked her magic, I was as cool, calm, and collected as a hippie on his herbal medicine. Understanding your spouse's sexual needs can make a world of difference between having sex and having great sex.

Having great sex is basically checking off all the boxes. Try to gain insight on what your spouse's boxes include. Once you realize what it is they like, try your best to make it happen. Keep in mind that people are exposed to different things in their life. Those things may become fantasies for them. Your spouse, as well as you, have certain passions and desires. The goal is to meet each other's expectations in the bedroom. I am aware that certain things may be a "no-no" for you or your spouse to do. If that is the case, try not to pressure them into doing something that they are not comfortable with. Be understanding. After all, it is your fantasy and not theirs. I would encourage both of you to be open to one another's desires. If it doesn't jeopardize your marriage, health, or spiritual relationship with God, consider it! The aim should be to please one another in such a way that neither of you will have to look outside of your bedroom for sexual fulfillment.

As I stated earlier in this book, people change. The spouse you married will not be the same person years from now. As people experience life, they tend to grow and evolve. Even taste buds change after a while. You probably can think of something you didn't like to eat as a child but love now as an adult, or vice-versa. So it is with sexual desires. They have a tendency to change over time. As the body changes, one may find certain areas more stimulating than others. To be honest, it just may be you trying different things that make your special person realize that they have a "new thing," and you'll know if they like it because they'll tell you, "Hey, do that 'lil thing' again." Then boom! You will realize that you have unlocked another box. I don't know if it is a guy thing or what, but fellas love to make their woman feel something that she has never felt before. Protecting her, providing for her, and pleasing her will make her crazy about you forever. Ladies, if you show him admiration, appreciation, and "sexual" action, he'll put you in the spot next to Jesus.

Some may want to know what to do if the thrill fades due to unforeseen circumstances. For many couples, this is a real issue. Of course, it's commonly talked about how at some point older men develop an erection problem, but it's not always the man with the issue. Women can also develop sexual dysfunction. I'm not a medical doctor so I will leave the majority of this content to the experts. My job here is to make suggestions and hopefully you and/or your spouse can find solutions. If arousal is an issue that is not medical-related for either party, it may be beneficial to see a sex therapist. Sex therapists have a tendency of helping couples rekindle the fire and passion that they once had. If the issue is related to a medical condition, then a doctor should be seen. Whatever you do, do something rather than nothing and allow that part of the fling to fade. At some point, maybe you and your spouse may decide that you both are cool without sex and still have a great working relationship. If that's the case, there's nothing wrong with that because it's mutual. Until that is the case, keep on striving to fulfill one another's sexual desires.

9 CHAPTER NINE:
Home Structure / Leadership/ Submission

This is a very important subject and cannot be ig-
nored. I am a God-fearing and Bible believing man,
so of course I'll have to take to the Word of God for this.
After all, this is a book based on Christian principles.
Many people have different views on what home structure
should look like. I refer to 1 Corinthians 11:2 as a foundation for believers with this teaching. Paul acknowledges
that Christ is the head of every man and that the man is
the head of the woman. The man was created first at crea-
tion and then the woman. He was not created for her, but
she was created for him. As a matter of fact, she was made
from the man. Read Genesis 2:15-24 for more clarity. So,
the home structure should consist of the authority order
descending from Christ, husband, wife, child. If a person
has a problem with this, then they have a problem with the
Word of God.

Many marriages have a problem with lasting because
there is a struggle with the leadership of the home. I must
say this first. God is the same today as He was yesterday.
He changes not, so He'll be the same forever. With that
being said, His ways always have and will always be the
same. I had to mention that because in recent years, some
cultures seem to have switched the headship of the household. The "independent" woman mentality has threatened

the chain of command in some homes. Headship is not determined by financial status, physical strength, or by how much education a person has, but it is determined by what the Word says. It's a blessing that women are able to experience having more wealth, health, and education, but at the end of the day, she is still the weaker vessel according to the Bible. In no way is this chapter to downgrade or belittle the woman. It's not to make her inadequate or insignificant. This chapter is here simply to help couples understand the structure that God put in place in the beginning.

I'm sure your pastor or spiritual covering does an excellent job teaching you and your family about how to effectively follow Christ. Therefore, I won't get in depth about that here. However, my goal is to help you and your spouse understand the importance of following God's divine order for the household. When things are in order, they flow more smoothly. I want your home to have peace and experience the blessings of God that come from having things in the right order. As we have established, the man should be the head of the house. Now, fellas, this doesn't give us the right to mistreat anyone or to have people thinking they are our slaves or minions. I have found that many women have a hard time following a man or submitting to a man who is not exemplifying the characteristics of a leader as described by the Bible. To be honest, this type of complaint always puts me in a pickle when trying to counsel couples. I do preach and teach that the man is the head of the household, but when the wife states that it is difficult for her to submit to a man or follow him when he is out of alignment with God, I can't fault her for feeling like that. It's really hypocritical to want her to fall in line when the man is out of line. Therefore, it would benefit everyone if the man would lead by example, by being in his rightful place.

As the head, the man should be willing to be the provider and the protector of his family. Even if the wife makes more money than he does, he should still have the innate drive to make things happen for the welfare of his family. He should carry the vision for the home. Not saying that the wife doesn't have input or say-so, I'm just saying that the man should be able and prepared to use wisdom and prudence to make the final call when it comes to making tough decisions concerning the home and family. Just to name a few things: he should lead the family to and in worship; make sure everyone's needs are met (whether physical, mental, emotional or spiritual); he should be wise with the household's finances, and if the family needs to make a major move or purchase, the responsibility is definitely placed upon him to make the best call possible. After all, the vision for the family rests upon him. Therefore, it is imperative for the man to stay prayerful and open to the voice of God for direction, so that he doesn't jeopardize the wellbeing of his family. I have found that certain habits and addictions of men have been known to compromise the overall standing of the household. Men, I can't stress this enough. Love your family more than any of the traps that are set out to entangle you, because once they entangle you, it is very possible that your family will be next.

The wife has a very important part to play in the home structure as well. As Proverbs 14:1 states, "Every wise woman buildeth up her house: but the foolish [woman] plucketh it down with her hands." Women, your husband will need you to assist him in assuring the family's success. As I've encouraged the man to not put his family in jeopardy, I encourage you likewise. Women, whether you know it or not, your place in the home is very significant. God created Eve for Adam because it was not good for him to be alone. Therefore, the Lord created Eve to be a helpmate for Adam. I like to put it this way: will you help him become better, or help him become bitter? Ladies, you do have that influence whether you know it or not. So try your best to bring comfort to the home rather than contention. I can assure you that being a contentious woman will only make things complicated. The Bible says, "It is better to dwell in the wilderness than with a contentious and an angry woman." It also says, "It is better to dwell in a corner of the housetop, than with a brawling woman in a wide house." So, ladies, remember, men have enough to fight with in the street; please don't make him have to come home and fight with you too. If you ever wonder why he's out with the guys a lot or in his man-cave often or just out doing things to avoid coming home, it just might be because you have a tendency of disrupting his peace with arguments and fights. Your aim should be to assist your husband as he is led by God to lead the family. Make the load lighter for him if possible because the burden of carrying the home can be a tedious task.

If I may, let's talk about submitting and all it entails. Ephesians 5:22 says, "Wives submit yourselves unto your own husbands, as unto the Lord." Wives, you have the responsibility as mandated by the Word of God to submit to your husband. The word submit in this particular scripture means to obey him. I hope you didn't cringe when you read that. I say that because over the years, I have found this conversation to be a touchy subject for a lot of headstrong women. There is nothing wrong with a woman being strong, but sometimes being headstrong can be problematic for a man. A man needs his woman to be submissive to him as he is the priest of his home. Over the years, I've witnessed many men develop a disdain for church or the pastor, all because their wives had a greater reverence for the preacher or submitted more to the preacher than they did to their own husband. So let me say to all the wives, please make sure you put no one else above your husband. The Lord is the only one that should have more admiration than your husband. Also, let me say this to all the husbands, please make sure you are in your rightful place to ensure that your wife doesn't develop the need or desire to place another man before you.

So, what does submitting actually look like? It's being supportive of your husband's decisions for the household without griping or attacking. That's not saying that you can't pose questions. Maybe there's something you don't understand or agree with that he's doing and need to get more clarity about. It is okay to ask questions—after all, the Bible does say, "In all thy getting, get an understanding." Fellas, please don't have a "don't question me" mentality. That type of mentality will only make the wife feel insignificant and without a voice. It will also eventually lead to some form of disconnect within the relationship. Guys, be willing to discuss your rationale behind the decisions that you are asking your family to follow. Even if it is saying, "Honey, I don't have all the answers right now. I'm just trusting God with this move." That is better than giving no explanation at all. Okay, back to what submitting looks like. It's being subject unto him. In this sense, the husband is over his wife. I hope that statement didn't ruffle any feathers. I don't mean that he's a slave owner or anything. It means that the hierarchy or chain of command starts with him. He should have the last say when it comes to the direction of the home. So, men, please do everything in your power to lead your family in a very successful way.

10   CHAPTER TEN: 4 C'S
The 4 C's of O.M.I.T.

I pray that our journey so far in this book has been very engaging and informative. Each chapter was designed to share insight on common problems that couples face. I carefully suggested practical solutions with Christian principles that could help you become victorious over these issues. I also pray that my experiences helped or will help your marriage. Now, finally, the whole purpose behind this book is this particular chapter. It holds the main keys to overcoming marital issues. I call these keys 4 C's of O.M.I.T. You can apply these C's to any of the problems mentioned in the previous chapters. The 4 C's are **Communicate, Confront, Compromise,** and **Conquer**. Hopefully, with each arising issue, the 4 C's of O.M.I.T. will help promote the balance, unity, and satisfaction needed to sustain a happy and healthy marriage.

Communicate! Talk about it! Communication is very essential. If one is bothered by an action of a spouse or situation, he or she should maturely express it to the other. It is not wise to assume that the spouse automatically knows of each time he or she may offend the other or if something is wrong. Therefore, if you are the one with the complaint, don't hold it in and let the pressure of it build up. However, try not to voice how you feel when you are angry—although that may be hard to do sometimes. It is usually beneficial to wait until you are calm to state how you feel. That way your spouse will be more receptive and not defensive. No one likes to be yelled at—especially grown folks. Treat the matter like you would want your spouse to treat a matter with you. It's usually easier to relay your message when you have a level head and have taken the time to carefully think about what it is exactly that you want to say. Being angry and lashing out complaints has a tendency to complicate things. Take it from me, some words you blurt out of anger can't be taken back. I've been there many times and regret it to this day. Love your spouse enough to communicate with them in a gentle way. A union where loves is the foundation should motivate both of you to be understanding and transparent with each other.

If you are the one who is on the other end of the complaint, you should listen to your mate and be considerate of his or her grievance. Try not to downplay or disregard how they feel. I didn't always listen well, and it cost me. Don't let it cost you! Active listening is a part of effective communication. Be careful to not listen, only to respond with a rebuttal. When the love of your life is expressing themselves, you should listen to comprehend. Once the complaint has been voiced and understood, the next step is the second C, Confront it.

Confronting it means to face it and deal with it. Just as it is important to discuss an issue, it is also important to deal with it. Talking about the issues alone will not help solve them. It can be very frustrating for a spouse to repeatedly express his or her concern to the other and have nothing done to alleviate the problem. Do not ignore your mate. If he or she is constantly venting out the same complaint, take heed and prepare yourself to deal with the matter—after all, you did vow to ensure the happiness of your significant other. If I can offer a word of advice from experience, please don't feel like you have a lot of time to deal with the complaints. You should be willing to handle the matter as soon as your spouse brings the complaint to you, especially if you know that the grievance is legitimate. Your partner will eventually get tired of voicing the same thing to you and will become silent. I'm a witness to some dangerous doors being opened when silence enters the picture. When your partner becomes silent about things that usually have them in their feelings, it can sometimes indicate that they've become numb to it or someone or something else is filling in the gap for you (neither scenario is good). Therefore, make it your business to face and deal with the complaint. So, how should you deal with it? Good question. That brings us to our next C, Compromise.

Compromise means to give and/or take to fix a problem. Sometimes compromising is all that stands in the way between the problem and solution. Compromising is said to be the secret to a happy marriage. One should not feel as though he or she has to be the one to give up everything or take everything in order for the other mate to be happy. If so, this can trigger the passive mate to feel depression and resentment. Most people who seek attention from someone outside of their marriage usually do so as a result of being vulnerable. In other words, their needs are not met at home, and for another to come along and present what the spouse is not giving can be very enticing. Most cases of infidelity are the outcomes of neglect and failure to resolve the revolving issues. You should willingly cooperate and make positive changes to ensure the success of your marriage. I plead with you to be willing to give what needs to be given of you and take what you need to take in order to fix your marriage. When I say give and take, I don't mean give or take abuse or disrespect. You may have to give up some pride or a way that you normally do things for the sake of fixing an issue that may pose a threat to your marriage. Remember, just because you have always done things a certain way, that doesn't mean that you have to always do them that way. Compromising just simply means adjusting the way you do things to find the common ground between you and your other half. After you set in your heart to compromise, the next step is the final C, Conquer the issue.

Conquering it means to overcome it. Once the issue has been acknowledged and faced and a plan has been set in motion to fix it, the couple should be well on their way to omitting (intentionally leaving out) that particular issue from their marriage. You conquer the issue by going through with the plan you both agreed upon to alleviate the problem. Once the plan is successful, put the issue behind you. Also know that it's okay to acknowledge the victory over a situation. That way you both can be aware of your marital victories. However, remain vigilant because if you both are not careful, past issues will resurface.

Holy matrimony will always have an enemy. Satan will try to attack your marriage every opportunity he gets, but as long as you allow God to help you, your marriage will be able to stand against the wiles of the devil. With that being said, it is imperative that once spouses fix an issue, that they do not allow it to cause any future distractions or divisions. A true sign of marital maturity is seen when spouses are able to move beyond former problems. Be mindful to know that either your issues will conquer your marriage, or your marriage will conquer the issues. Keep calm and O.M.I.T., my friends.

"...EITHER YOUR ISSUES WILL CONQUER YOUR MARRIAGE OR YOUR MARRIAGE WILL CONQUER YOUR ISSUES."

MARITAL PRAYER

Heavenly Father, I come to you as your humble servant on behalf of all ordained marriages. Keep your hedge of protection around them, Lord. I pray that you bless each couple that's reading this book with wisdom, knowledge, and understanding that will help them overcome the many challenges of marriage. I pray that you bless their home with peace, love, and unity. I pray for their health, wealth, and success. Heal where there has been hurt and traumatic experiences. Teach them how to forgive and move on while reestablishing their trust in one another. Rekindle the fire between those who have lost it, oh God, and restore the love between them that bonded them together in the first place. I pray that you bind the hand of the enemy so that he cannot put asunder that which you have put together. Incline your ear, oh Lord, to the prayers of husbands and wives who are crying out to you for help with their marriage. Let them know that you are yet with them and have not forsaken them. Make known unto them what it is that you would have them to do for your glory. Be merciful, Lord, and forgive them of their trespasses. I pray that you help the men to be godly husbands and the women to be virtuous wives. Please let this book be a blessing and a powerful resource to the readers, for I have done what you have led me to do. Let them learn from my experiences and build upon the knowledge that I have shared. As I close this prayer, I ask that you equip the couple that's reading this book with the keys to overcome any and every obstacle that they may face. Give them grace, Lord, and continue to bless them with your favor. In Jesus' name I pray. Amen!

NOTES